GRACEFUL GRATITUDE

A Book of Holiday Graces

Elizabeth Michele Cantine

4ARTS EDUCATION PRESS

Graceful Gratitude: A Book of Holiday Graces

Elizabeth Michele Cantine

Paperback Edition: ISBN-10:173211630X
Paperback Edition: ISBN-13: 978-1-7321163-0-6

Library of Congress Control Number: 2018943099

Printed in USA

DEDICATION

To my incredible, inspiring, spirited, and spiritual *you are my sunshine* mother Amelia Abraham (Grandma, Nana, Great Nana, wife, sister, aunt) who was never too busy, too tired or too ill to say thank you. Her last words to us were: "Thank you - I love you".

And our sunshine faded…

CONTENTS

INTRODUCTION

Since God blessed me in so many ways and since I love to write, I began composing holiday graces to be shared with family and friends on these special days. Before the holiday meal, a family member or I would recite the grace. I would also email the grace to others as a warm greeting and an expression of my gratefulness. In turn, their responses deepened my thinking and thankfulness. We bonded during these special times. I hope my reflective writings to God grace you and yours during holidays and any day. I thank you for reading them and becoming part of my graceful gift of gratitude…

Chapter 1

EASTER GRACES

ELIZABETH M. CANTINE

Reaching Out

Dear Jesus,
As I interpret the cross
Your outstretched arms draw me in
But I realize they're not just extended towards me but to the world
To the seas of mysteries, to the mountains of miracles
To the deserts of despair, to the hills of hope
Your hands feel and heal, as our hands held at our hearts
Give You our love and reverence
In our crosses and in our losses
We remember those in Your Heavenly hold
Beloved parents, spouses, children, friends, soldiers, and heroes
Dear Jesus,
We thank You for embraces, for Earth, for Easter, for eternity…
Amen.

A Contemporary Grace

Jesus called me today
This is what He advised:
Walk behind me, I have cleared a path for compassion
Race in front of me, I designed the course
Chat with me, I am a good listener
Pray for those not here, for those who serve and sacrifice
Join my choir, I composed a song of hope
Be part of my circle of dance, I choreographed a work of love
Help me carry my cross, I will reciprocate
Celebrate with me, I planned a party which will last forever
Keep in touch...
We will through grateful hearts and faithful souls
Amen.

ELIZABETH M. CANTINE

Walking with You, Dear Lord

Inspired by walking with You, dear Jesus, on that Good Friday,
1965, in Jerusalem, the very steps of YOUR Way of the Cross.
Accompanied by my beloved parents and two of my Lebanese
cousins, we touched your Holy Sepulcher, we touched your
wooden cross...

Thank You, Jesus, for giving us the grace
Of walking with You today, stopping to reflect
Instead of racing through life in distracted disarray
Thank You for leading us on your course
To help those who have lost their way
To those who have nowhere to stay
To those who have no bread or wine
To those whose health and pain are maligned
To those soldiers who fight and die for us
To those family and friends who gave us life and lived for us
Thank you for leading us to FAITH
Death defied! Eternally we walk with You in prayer
Thank You for leading us to HOPE
Life anew! Eternally we walk with You in springtime air
Robins sing ALLELIUA; Rainbows echo AMEN!

ELIZABETH M. CANTINE

Colors and Crosses

Dear Lord,
We give You thanks for the colors of this season
And for crosses, crossings, and crossroads
We are grateful for your cross of hope, renewal, and rebirth
For the rewards and risks of crossings
For directing us at crossroads which we face
In health decisions, in work, in everyday life
And in new paths, as age might detour us
We give You thanks for the colors on our Easter table
And for coloring our lives with rainbows of riches
Amen.

ELIZABETH M. CANTINE

One Day

Dear Lord,
One day You broke bread at the table with those You loved
We are here today to thank You for our breaking bread with those
We love and those we loved who celebrate with You...
One day You picked up your cross with courage and faith
We are here today to thank You for picking up our crosses
And helping those who have no strength to bend down
One day You walked the via Dolorosa with compassion
Some of us have walked those very same steps
We are here today to thank You for The Passion
And to thank those who serve and those who have died for others
As we revere the Christ in them
One day You took your last breath on the cross
We are here today to thank You for your destined devotion
And for setting the whole world in a different motion
One day, the third day, You changed; we changed!
Alleluia! Amen.

Centered

Dear Jesus,
We thank You for being and bearing our cross
We ask You to guide us to where the crossed lines meet
One line from Earth to your hand
The other from Heaven to your feet.
At the center is reflection, redemption, and resurrection
Your immortal love
Please keep us centered in life with this image and strength
And help us bring others in at any great length
We thank You for centering us on this Easter Day
Bringing us in with loved ones in this special way
Amen.

That They May Have Life

Dear Lord,
As we embrace today your resurrection celebration
We thank You for your love of perfect oblation
As we give You our earthly pain and stress
We thank You for your comforting caress
As we remember our loved ones at Easters past
We thank You for their memories to last
As we see spring surrounding us with blessings untold
We thank You for all the beauty and blossoms which unfold
As we think of those who cannot see the flower
Or hear the song of bird
We thank You for sharing your faith
And spreading your word
As we hear your powerful message
Of passion and hope redundantly
"I came so that they may have life and have it abundantly"
Now and forever
Amen.

Earth, Wind, Fire, and Faith

Thank You, God, for the earth from which this meal came
Thank You for our worldly blessings
Too numerous to name.
Thank You for the wind which swirls our dreams around
Please give gusts to those whose feet fall on the ground.
Thank You for the fire from hearts of those we loved and love
For those souls no longer here
You're embracing from above...
Thank You for the roots which bore the tree
On which Christ died for You and me
A tree without branch or leaf
A cross which changed belief
Thank You for the faith which transcends reason
For the sacrifice and hope of this Easter Season
For sharing the Passion, then spiritual elation!
Forever living life with You in celebration!
Amen.

ELIZABETH M. CANTINE

Wonders

Thank You, Lord, for worldly wonders
For what is around us and for those who surround us
Thank You for earthly wonders
For warmth which encircles us and for beauty which engages us
Thank You for spiritual wonders
For that which gives us hope and for You who gives us life
For heartfelt wonders for those we love around us now
As for those beloved in our past around you now
We thank You for all we hold as wonder-filled and wonderful
While wondering why we are so blessed
Please bless those who have never seen the Easter Lilies
Or listened to the springtime birds, or held a precious pet
Or hugged a cherished child
Now reflecting on your will and wondrous love
We gratefully celebrate the wonderment
Of your resurrection and our eternal future
May the wonders live on!
Amen!

ELIZABETH M. CANTINE

Easter Presents

Dear God,
We thank you for Easter gifts of food, family, and friends
For our loved ones now with You whose spirits never end...
We are grateful for your presents by answering our prayers
For lightening a problem or heartbreak we cannot bear
You have taught us to compassionately carry our crosses
As You lift us from our falls and losses
We must unwrap more often every gift from You
Since You sacrificed the greatest gift to be born anew
Amen.

Chapter 2

THANKSGIVING GRACES

Never Out

Dear Lord, we give You thanks
For the feast on our table, encircled by family and friends we hold.
We give You thanks
For the feast at your table
Encircled by family and friends we miss
We give You thanks for your nourishment
When food is not enough.
We ask You to help us create
Out of crisis, crosses
Out of frustration, fraternity
Out of embers, embraces
Out of thoughtless taking, thanks of giving…
Amen.

God is Hosting

Did you receive God's invitation to Thanksgiving dinner?
He's invited all, the righteous and the sinner
Host gift is just to ask for mercy and offer thanks
And to remember the departed, the poor and the ill he's guested
He's worked so hard; He's never really rested
The favor of your reply is kindly requested
Amen.

We Thank Your Goodness

We thank you, God, for bounties and blessings
For melodies and miracles, for goods and goodness
For Your goodness we see in others everyday
In those who served and serve and sacrifice
We are grateful for Your goodness
We see in our families and friends
Those whom we revere and those whom we remember
There is goodness worth loving forever...
Amen.

ELIZABETH M. CANTINE

Hand to Heart

Dear Lord,
Hand to heart, our heads we bow
In thanks for family and friends and those with You now
Hand to heart, with health of body and strength of mind
We wish the same for all mankind
Hand to heart we give a quiet salute
For those who served and serve with praises mute
Hand to heart we touch pets and beasts in peaceful land
And are touched by blessings small and grand
Hand to heart our souls send grateful prayer
For feasts and fortunes beyond compare
Amen.

ELIZABETH M. CANTINE

Foremost Thanks

Dear Lord, on this Thanksgiving
We give thanks for turkey and dressing
For bounty and blessing
For family and friends whom we touch
For those whom we miss so very much...
For family and memorable tradition
For friends and pets – a fun addition!
For home and happy time
For travel and smiles sublime
For health and hope
For ways to cope
For goodness and good people's graces
For graceful art, sporting games and races
We give thanks for all that is around, for all we see above
And of all we share with others through eternal love
Amen.

ELIZABETH M. CANTINE

Here…

Dear Lord,
We thank You for our beginning, our beautiful birth Here
Not in a cave, nor a desert, nor a place of famine or fear
Blessed with peace of mind and safety surrounding us Here
We heartily thank all those who serve elsewhere
We thank you for memories now and always of those not Here
Whose love we treasure with a smile and tear
We thank You for what we feel, for what we see Here today
We thank You for family, friends, and feasts eternally!
Amen.

CANDLES AND FLOWERS

Inspired by the words of that young boy in Paris following another terrorist attack there.

For calm and faith, candles and flowers
Thank You, Lord, for the hours
For blossoms of blessings and bouquets of bounties
For faith to keep us strong
For caring for those for whom we long
For caressing us which keeps us bound
To enjoy the beauty all around
For comforting us with hope and might
With candles which protect and light
To see our way in the darkest night
Please pass Your Spirit and a few seeds
To those who serve; to those with needs
While our hearts and souls your mercy feeds
We thank you, Lord, for candles and flowers
For the love we share in our grateful hours
Amen.

Around, Abound!

Dear Lord,
You give us the quiet song of birds
Louder than our cheers and tears
You give us days of sun and dreams of hope brighter than our fears
You give us your gifts of Nature's awesome sight
And those whose human nature show us love and light
Please help those who hope for fullness and future bright
As we appreciate what we had and have, just look around!
Family, friends, pets, happy moments abound!
So we need to take a moment each day, as we should
To thank You for all that is right and for all that is good!
Amen.

ELIZABETH M. CANTINE

Fortunate

Dear Lord, we offer You thanks and remembrances
For feasting with family while others forage for food
For all we enjoy while others suffer
For all we celebrate while others cry
For all we have which others need
For all we see which others seek
For those who have passed
Whose shared love gilded and guided our past
For the present beauty and faith in our everyday life
Our devoted family and friends, a loving pet, a simple rose
An autumn leaf, a smile from the soul, an answered prayer
We, the faithful, the fortunate, offer You thanks
Amen.

ELIZABETH M. CANTINE

While

We thank You Lord on this gorgeous day of thanks
For filling our plates everyday with life's richness and realities
While so many hunger for life's substance and sustenance
We thank You for the privilege of togetherness
And sharing in celebration
While too many feel isolation and desolation
We thank you for the table you have spread before us
While we remember our loved ones not at this feast today
But whose love will always nourish us
We thank You while we enjoy our daily diet of blessings
Amen.

Your Ocean

Dear Lord,
We have the good fortune of gazing out the window and giving
Thanks for the
Waves of wonder
Bays of bounty
Harbors of health
Colors of calm
Storms of strength
Lulls of love
We ask You to guide those who are adrift or alone tonight
Tomorrow may they share in the ocean of abundance and hope
Over which we sail
Amen.

ELIZABETH M. CANTINE

Hand in Hand

Dear Lord,
Hand in hand
We stand around the Thanksgiving table
Holding, touching, bonding, reflecting
We are grateful to those whose hands of courage nourish us
We thank those whose hands of love have fed us
We thank You for our good food and fortunes which enable us
To assist those who need a hand out
Those who only have a handful of wheat or rice today
We pray for them, whose hands hungrily reach out
In need, in pain, in sorrow
May they feel your taking them hand in hand
Amen.

ELIZABETH M. CANTINE

Dichotomy

Dear Lord,
On this Thanksgiving
We reflect on the dichotomy of dispersion of your gifts
Our cultivated earth, the unseeded desert
Our winds of wonder, the hurricanes of horror
Our waters of life, the floods of drowning
Our flames which feed, the fires which starve
But we are filled with your goodness
So we give You thanks for
This table of feast
This tableau of family
This tablet of togetherness
This taste of infinity...
Amen.

Here and There

We thank You God today and everyday
For what is here and what is there
For food on this table
For the nourishment you give our hearts and souls
For those here and
For those there with You whom we remember and treasure
For those here around the table
For those there around the world
Who give us courage through their battles
With diseases, daily challenges, and terrorism
We are grateful here for family, friends, faith, and fun!
For roses, rainbows, and red ribbons there in the sunset…
Amen.

ELIZABETH M. CANTINE

The Old Elm Tree, 2006

I saw a special bird perched on my old Elm tree
I asked them both, what have you given me?
Some might scoff and simply say,
It's just a bird on a branch, so what's all the fuss?
But then we think of God and what He has given us
The trees, the plants, the fruits upon which we feast
The lightness on the wings, the burden on the beast
We give Him thanks for the evergreens
For earth and sun and nature's scenes
For calm around the changing leaves
While the windless world watches and grieves
As the leaves fall and fighting goes on
Among the fields of Iraq and the Cedars of Lebanon
We pray for those in the autumn of their lives
We pray for their spring where a blossom thrives
Today the bird flew away from my old Elm tree
But I thank God for the everlasting memory...
Amen.

Your Pilgrims

We thank You Lord for the wealth in the clouds' silver lining
Though others remain poor in the pounding storms
We thank you for the legs of light and life which stretch
Down to dance on the ocean's crest
Though others are bound or dying in its depths
We thank you for the fullness of the lone sailboat on the horizon
Though the lonely sailor hungers
We admire the sun and moon reflecting their circles on the water
Where on different tangents, Pilgrims and Indians encircled the
Feast and gave thanks as we do now
Amen.

ELIZABETH M. CANTINE

Memories

Dear Lord, our prayer of gratitude does not need to rhyme
Though thanks and thoughtfulness chime in time
We thank You for the feast today and the banquet beyond
For those we remember in other homes and in your forever bond
We thank You for giving them to us and memories fond
Of Thanksgivings together shared and traditions set
With hearts filled with generous love with no regret
Amen.

Out of

Dear Lord,
We give thanks
For the feast on our table
Encircled by family and friends we hold
We give thanks
For the feast at your table
Encircled by family and friends we miss
We give thanks
For your nourishment when food is insufficient
We ask You to help us create
Out of crises, crosses
Out of frustration, fraternity
Out of embers, embraces
Out of thoughtless taking, thanks of giving
Amen.

ELIZABETH M. CANTINE

Daily Bread

Dear Lord,
We thank You for giving us our daily bread
For the abundance in the days before and those ahead
For the days and nights of good health
For the food for our hearts so we can love and feel
For the manna for our souls so we can observe
The outlines of the islands
Then dancing dabs of sunlight on the ocean
The warm canyons in the clouds at dusk
Rainbows through which we run, sail, and fly!
We thank You for giving us our daily bread
For the abundance in the days before and those ahead
Amen.

ELIZABETH M. CANTINE

To and Taken

We thank you God today and everyday
For bestowing material blessings and comforts
For those who bless our lives
For those You have given to us
For those You have taken from us
For all our Thanksgiving happiness today
For all our daily disappointments You help us conquer
For this and that and everything we touch and use
For taking away all at the end except for Your promise
Amen.

Thanks for the Day

Dear Lord,
Each morning we awake to another day of living
Thanking You for all You gave and for all You are giving
Blessing us to be born in this beautiful place
Distant from wars of religion and race
To those who serve, please grant them grace
We thank You for the day
So we can pursue our passion and race in the dark
So we can dream to the stars and walk in the park
So we can view Nature's vistas and hear music in trees
So we can engage with people and pets for forever memories
As we remember those from the past with a smile and tear
Through the love we shared, they will always be near
We thank You for the day, this day especially
So we can together give you thanks for the feast eternally
Amen.

Us

Dear Lord,
There are so many things we need to thank You for
Every day, everywhere, we take so much for granted
But we need to realize You granted these for us
We, who are not worthy, but we understand
There are things worth dying for
In those who face or fight adversity
There are things worth living for
In those who work, parent, teach, coach, or serve
There are things worth being patient for
In those who care and cure
There are things worth more than we could ever value
For you lived and died for
Us
Amen.

Our Giving God

The table's full, we've prepared the feast
We give thanks to our giving God
With friends and family, our hearts complete
Though we're left an empty seat
For our loved ones departed but forever near
For those today who live in uncertainty and fear
For those who live in pain and despair
So we all somehow share the empty chair
As your will fulfills us every day, everywhere
In ways we both lament and laud
We give thanks to our giving God
Amen.

Sensitive

Dear Lord,
On this day of gratitude
As we thank You for gratifying our senses
Help us listen to the sensible
And be sensitive to the senseless
As together we hear
The calm of fulfillment
The cry of hunger
The whisper of peace
The deafening of battle
The dialogue of caring
The silence of soliloquy
We are the fortunate, the grateful, the receptive
We hear Your music
Please share the symphony
Amen.

Graced

Dear Lord, we thank You for the grace
And good life in which we are cast
We thank those who have graced our lives now and in the past
We thank You for allowing us to gracefully both
Sail and stall, flower and fall
We thank You for your gracious light each day
While others lost in the dark cannot find their way
We thank You for the graciousness
We feel from family and friends
And for love we share, the love God sends
Amen.

The Modern Age

Dear Lord,
We are twirling and whirling in this Modern Age
The 21st century of technological wisdom and sage
So much to do, trying to manage stress
But we need to take a breath and do much less
So we can focus on mediation and prayer
Feeling your love and trust, it is everywhere!
We must allot time each day, not just on this Thanksgiving
To offer our gratitude to the One who blesses our living
Please let us never be too advanced or modern
To appreciate and apply what we can learn
From You
Amen.

Chapter 3

CHRISTMAS GRACES

HOLY NIGHT

Dear Lord,
Thanks for the Holy Night of our first Christmas Eve
For the humanity in your birth, the message you leave
Thanks for the celebration and the traditions which followed
For those in our hearts in Christmas memories hallowed
Please keep them safe with you and help those mortals on Earth
Who doubt the story of your birth
Dismissing it as merely myth or mirth
With You, we will remind them there are times
We can fall on the ground or fall on our knees
Following with faith, singing with hope, praying tonight
We believe, oh holy day, oh holy night
Amen.

(following this grace, we listen to "Oh, Holy Night" and reflect...)

ELIZABETH M. CANTINE

Christmas Past, Christmas Future

On this commemoration and celebration of Jesus' nativity
We give thanks Lord for the fullness of the festivity
Though on the Eve and Day we think of moments of the past
With family and friends - memories which last...
We thank You for those we loved who guided and gave
And for those traditions which live long past the grave
We acknowledge change and challenges we sometimes dread
But with faith and hope
You remind us to look back as we look ahead
Amen.

ELIZABETH M. CANTINE

Christmas Carol Notes

Dear Lord, we reflect and take note
A Child is Born – let us cradle the starving and forlorn
Away in a Manger – let us hold close the homeless, the stranger
Silent Night, Holy Night – let us keep our departed loved ones in
Your light
Oh, Come All Ye Faithful – to those of no or different faith
Let us be mindful
God Rest Ye Merry Gentlemen – to those in any battle
Let us pray for peace of mind and peace amen
As we fall on our knees, let us thank You for lifting us up
And for leading the choir of angels to sing
Joy to the World, let Earth receive her King!
Amen.

In...

Dear Jesus, in prayer, our heads we bow
To thank you for blessings then and now
For colored lights and candles' scent
For family traditions and what it meant
To celebrate with loved ones no longer by the tree
To keep them so alive in heartfelt memory...
Dear Jesus, in hope, help us soar to your star
Though the sun's light might often seem afar
Dear Jesus, in faith, let us be strong
Sharing kindness, knowing right from wrong
Dear Jesus, in Your birth, you gave us Christmas gifts
To dance to angels' voices, our spirit lifts
So we give You thanks for this special meal and Eve
And for allowing us to share gifts of love before we leave
Amen.

ELIZABETH M. CANTINE

Amen, Amen.

Thanks, dear Jesus, for the star on Christmas Eve
For brightening times when we despair or grieve
Thanks for the simple manger and
For saving us from imagined danger
Thanks for Mary and Joseph at your side
For parents and family who lovingly guide
Thanks for sleeping in peace and wakening our souls
So we can live out our dreams and realize our goals
Thanks for the gifts of the Three Wise Men
For the lessons of giving, Amen, Amen.

The Simple, The Faithful

The glare from computer screens, cities, and freeways,
Thank You, God, for the faithful flame of a candle
The complexity, the intrigue, the infinity of galaxies
Thank You, God, for the faithful focus to one star
The shopping, the lists, the lines, the frustration
Thank You, God, for the faithful gifts of the Wise men
The planning, the parties, the trips, the celebrations
Thank You, God, for the lasting memory of the manger
The questionings, the setbacks, the disappointments,
Thank You, God, for the faithful birth of your Son
Who we pray will always give us hope, peace, and a faithful
Merry Christmas
Amen.

In Concert

Dear God,
We thank You for the gifts around the tree of living
For family and friends and our shared love of giving
We thank You for miracles in each day
Please listen as we pray
For those we love who have passed
As our minds and hearts hold them fast
As we pray for restored health
Realizing there is no greater wealth
We thank You for the hope and light
For well-being and clear sight
For this wondrous, star filled eve
To restore our faith to believe
That with us, your angels dance and sing
In concert to your everything
Amen.

Goodwill and Peace

Dear Lord, we thank You for blessings and our plates that You fill
Particularly on this Christmas Day we look for peace and goodwill
We thank You for the peace in our heart and soul
As we ask You to help those whose daily duress has taken its toll
We thank You for the security and peace we enjoy
As we ask You to help those in conflict who wander with no joy
We thank You for the service of those just next door
As we ask You to guide those fighting in a no win war
Help us celebrate the goodness of those secret Santas in a store
And those who practice kindness and courtesy as it was before
Those who volunteer to pay pet adoption fees during holidays
Those who volunteer to assist the homeless and at toy giveaways
Our friends and family who greet us with a smile and gifts of caring
Bless them and our departed, spread your peace and love
Within us and without on the wings of a dove
So that Your willingness to sacrifice from your human birth
Gives meaning to goodwill and "Peace on Earth"
Amen.

Merry Moments

We thank You Lord for this meal
For this merry day and eve we celebrate with bliss
With those around us, remembering those we miss
Merry moments of the past; merry moments now to last
We thank You for family and friends all together – what a gift!
As traditions with love give our hearts and souls a spiritual lift!
We keep mindful of the miraculous manger
As we fret and focus about worldly danger
We thank You for our safety and for those who served and serve
For those who sacrifice with courage, strength, and verve
We thank You for the carols and your story
Reminding us of your grace and glory!
But how can we ever show you our gratitude – we have so much!
While there are so many in need of your comforting touch
Please bless those who do not have merry moments this holiday
Please help us share our grateful presents of good fortune
Health, laughter, awe, adventures, pets, surprises, love, and faith
These moments make merry Christmas and merry forever…
Amen.

ELIZABETH M. CANTINE

Mirror

Dear Jesus,
I noticed a mirror wrapped with a red bow hanging on a wall
A metaphor for You, a perfect present, reflecting all
As we look in it, what do we think, what do we see
The Christ in everyone; the Christ in me
All which You have given us, every possession, child, and pet
Thank you, God,
For what we have, for those we've loved and those we've met
And for the greatest gift of your Son on Earth
So today we can honor your Christ child's birth
We mortals who get so wrapped up in holiday preparation
We tend to neglect the meaning of His birthday celebration
We may forget how His life matured from Mary's maternity
To that hanging mirror so that it's Christmas for eternity
Amen.

Christmas Reflections

Dear Lord,
Last night I reflected on what faith meant to me
A mélange of mystery, miracle, and love
A combination of fate and fact
I cannot touch it or taste it
But I can see it in others and in daily events
I can feel it
I can hear it – "Do you hear what I hear?"
Thank You for bounties and blessings, "Joy to the World"
For those who bless our lives, "Oh, come all ye faithful"
For those who have blessed us, "Angels we have heard on high"
For calm and caring – "Goodwill to men"
For whisper of peace, "Whisper, a tiny baby is born tonight"
But for those less fortunate we hear
The cry of hunger, "The silent Word is pleading"
The deafening of battle, "Fall on your knees"
The prayers of the ill, "How still we see thee lie"
The silence of solitude, "Silent Night, Holy night"
So thanks be to God, we are celebrating, "Deck the Halls"
We hear your song, "And Heavn' and Nature sing"
We sing in the choir, "Christ our Savior is born!"
Amen.

Heavenly

Dear Jesus,
On the Eve of Your birthday we thank You for food and family
For being together so that we remember that
Your birth and death gave us the greatest gift – Heaven!
And the worldly gifts you have so generously bestowed
Are heavenly words: Health, Healing, Help, Hope, and Happiness
We thank You for these heavenly presents we enjoy today
And ask that You please remember those who live
Without these and embrace them and us tonight
As we thank You for heavenly days now and
Our truly heavenly days ahead
Amen.

Three Candles

Whether it was Star of David or a comet
We celebrate the light; we celebrate the night
We thank You God for the hope (as we light first candle)

Whether or not Immaculate Conception
Is something we can understand
When we see a mother hold her child's hand
We celebrate bonds; we celebrate love
We thank You God for family (as we light second candle)

Whether we marvel or mourn at the young boy who preached
Himself to the cross
We celebrate life; we celebrate life after death
We thank You God for faith (as we light third candle)

On this special Eve we ask You Lord to help those
Who have no hope, no family, no faith
No candles to light on Christmas or any day
As we thank You for lighting our candles of Christmas everyday
And sharing eternally in Your Happy Birthday
Amen.

Chapter 4

ANY DAY GRACES

ELIZABETH M. CANTINE

Daybreak

(Composed from actual events and inspirations, 2010)

One night I couldn't see the moon behind the clouds
One day I couldn't see God behind the crowds
Of the criminals, of the dying, and those who doubt
Questioning what faith is all about
Then at dark, the moon miraculously appeared full
It was there all along; I was wrong
At church, the thought I had long kept only in my mind
Was there on the screen, and ringing in song
"I can't imagine life without God"
Raise our hands, hear us applaud!
Our belief and commitment we must cherish
For His plan shall not perish
Not in darkness, not in doubt
But lives in the daybreak of our real tomorrow
Amen.

Across and Farther

Dear Lord,
We go across the street to reach our destination
We've gone across the river to the north and emancipation
We've become cross in matters of consternation
We've been at crossroads in perplexed contemplation
So we thank You Lord
When You divert us from danger
When You navigate our waters
When You calm our anger
When You direct us as your sons and daughters
When You carry us across and farther
Amen.

ELIZABETH M. CANTINE

Simple Thanks

We thank you God for food, family, and friends
For both presents concealed and those daily revealed
Through memories and miracles
And in our troubled times in our media and story
You give us hope, strength, and glory
Amen.

Belief

Dear Lord,
We thank You for your gifts and graces of
Sunrises of hope, sunsets of comfort, showers of renewal
Bouquets of memories, waterfalls of reflections
Yellow daffodils of fun, breezes of love
Melodies of birds eternally happy
Because BELIEF is in the air!
Amen.

For This

Dear Lord,
For this day we are grateful
For this food we are thankful
Please bless each family member and friend
Please bless those who cannot fend
Amen.

ELIZABETH M. CANTINE

Old and New

(I recited first verse as a child; I recite second verse as an adult.)

Dear God,
Thank you for the morning light
For health and strength and loving care
Thank You for this food we share

Thank You for the dark at night
For rest and time to unwind
We give You our heart and mind
Amen.

ELIZABETH M. CANTINE

Tables Turned

Dear Jesus,
Thank You for blessing my meals at the table
And for allowing me to turn the tables
On a special day, birthday, holy day, holiday, every day
To think of what I might do to earn your grace
For living life as You meant it to be
In a generous, grateful, graceful way
Amen.

Acknowledgements

My mother Amelia, father Mitchell, my big brother Art, sister Diane, brother Mike, and paraplegic Uncle Al for raising me and reminding me to be appreciative and to say "Thank you".

My husband Richard Alanson Cantine for his constant support, advice, assistance, and proofreading.

Our son Thomas Mitchell, daughter-in-law Miranda Simone, and grandchildren Sophia Amelia, Aidan Michael and Maya Hanni for their excitement and encouragement on my becoming an author.

To all my family members, Goddaughters, in-laws, friends, colleagues, students, and Ready Willing and Able families who have read, commented, and enriched my graces.

To my church family at St. Francis Episcopal Church for their faith and inspiration to help me reflect and remember.

Beth K. Whittenbury, author of *How to Self Publish a Book in 10 Easy Steps: A Guide for Authors Who Want to Publish Their Books For Free* and publishing consultant, fellow tapper, and friend who made my dream of publishing my book a reality through her expertise, her talents, and her instructive book!

ABOUT THE AUTHOR

Elizabeth Michele Cantine, a native Californian and graduate from UCLA, has spent her career of over 50 years as a classroom and dance educator. She has written and presented many units integrating the fine arts into the K-12 curriculum, many of them based on poetry. She was an LA Music Center Arts Education Bravo Award Finalist and served many years as President of California Dance Educators Association. When Liz was four, her always thoughtful and thankful Lebanese-American mother took her to church, to kindergarten, and to a dance lesson. Each of these childhood firsts fueled her early excitement and later passion in religion, education, and dance. From first grade, Liz always enjoyed writing, especially poetry. In the future, she plans to publish her books on poetry about famous artists and people, poems to family and friends, and her two children's books. She can be reached via email at dancinliz@aol.com

NOTES

GRACEFUL GRATITUDE

ELIZABETH M. CANTINE